A LITTLE
Texas
Cookbook

Carolyn Dehnel

ILLUSTRATED BY
SUE DRAY

Chronicle Books

First published in 1992 by
The Appletree Press Ltd,
7 James Street South, Belfast BT2 8DL.
Copyright © 1992 The Appletree Press, Ltd.
Illustrations © 1992 Sue Dray used under
Exclusive License to
The Appletree Press, Ltd.

First published in the United States in 1992 by
Chronicle Books, 275 Fifth Street,
San Francisco, CA 94103

ISBN 0-8118-0114-4

9 8 7 6 5 4 3 2

Introduction

Six flags have flown over Texas — Spanish, French, Mexican, Republic of Texas, Confederate and Old Glory. As far as food is concerned, the range of influences is even wider. What has left the strongest mark? The Old South with its traditions of hospitality and good and plentiful food? The cowboy with his chuck wagon? The frontier with its privations and plain food? Mexico with its chillies and corn? Or the later immigrants — English, German, Greek, Czech, and Danish? Around Dallas, the Southern tradition prevails, with its luscious fruits, nut pies and cobblers, fresh garden produce, fried meats, poultry and fish. In East Texas the French influence spills over from Louisiana with its Creole/Cajun traditions. In South and West Texas, Mexican cooking, using corn and a wide variety of beans, is widespread.

Texas cooking, of whatever variety, calls for fresh ingredients, generous helpings, and a welcome for what is original and new. Many of the recipes in this book make large quantities of food, party-size portions, and are a reflection of the welcome that awaits any unexpected guest. There is always a place at the table for the stranger.

A note about cornmeal — it is the result of grinding corn/maize. *It is not cornflour!* Italian polenta makes an acceptable substitute if cornmeal is not available.

A note on measures

Spoon measures are level. All recipes are for four unless indicated.

Starters

Spicy Cheese Balls

Created in Monterey, California, by a man named Jack — or so the story goes — Monterey Jack is essential in Tex-Mex cooking.

¹/₂ cup finely grated Monterey Jack cheese or mild cheddar	¹/₂ tsp hot chilli powder
	¹/₂ cup chopped walnuts
¹/₂ cup blue cheese	pinch Cayenne pepper
¹/₂ cup cream cheese	**Garnish**
1 tbsp butter	chilli powder
¹/₂ tsp Worcestershire sauce	chopped parsley

(serves 10–12)

Blend the three cheeses with butter, Worcestershire sauce, chilli powder, walnuts, and Cayenne. Shape into a ball. Roll in extra chilli powder and then the chopped parsley. Refrigerate overnight. Allow to come to room temperature for 30 minutes. Serve with snack crackers.

Green Chilli Dip

A very mild chilli used in Mexican cooking gives a delicate flavor to this dip. It's best eaten a day after preparation.

8 oz cream cheese	3 tbsp finely chopped onion
3 tbsp mayonnaise	1 tsp lemon juice
4 oz can chopped green chillies	dash Tabasco
	hot paprika

Blend the cream cheese and mayonnaise. Mix in the rest of the ingredients except the paprika. Chill overnight. Sprinkle with paprika and serve with crudités or tortilla chips.

Texas Caviar

All over Texas, the centerpiece of the New Year's Day meal is a bowl of black-eyed peas. Eating black-eyed peas on January 1 ensures good luck in the coming year.

2 1/2 pts cooked black eye beans	1/2 tsp salt
1 cup corn oil	2 cloves garlic
1/4 cup cider vinegar	1 red onion, thinly sliced
1 tsp dry mustard powder	salt, pepper

Drain liquid from beans. Make a vinaigrette with the oil, vinegar, mustard powder, and salt. Mix together the beans, garlic, onions, and seasoning. Pour the vinaigrette over and store in an air tight container for three days in the refrigerator. Remove the garlic. Serve as either a salad or a pickle. Will keep up to two weeks if kept refrigerated.

Jalapeño Jelly

Although filled with very hot jalapeño peppers, this jelly has a sweet/sour taste. Use canned, pickled peppers.

8–10 jalapeño peppers with seeds, ground
5 oz green or red pepper, deseeded and ground
1 1/2 cups cider vinegar
6 1/2 cups granulated sugar
bottle Certo or liquid pectin
green or red food coloring (optional)

Mix peppers, vinegar, and sugar in a large pot. Bring to a rolling boil, ensuring that sugar dissolves. Boil for 8 minutes. Remove from heat and add Certo or liquid pectin. Stir well. Cool slightly and pour into sterilized and warmed jelly jars. Cover and seal with vinegar proof lids. Serve with cold meats. To serve as part of an hors d'oeuvres, pour the jelly over a block of cream cheese on a large plate. Serve with snack crackers.

Red Beans and Rice Soup

Bean soups are typical of Southwestern cooking and are especially good for lunch or supper on a cold day on the plains. The addition of the rice is an influence from Louisiana-Cajun cooking.

1 cup pinto beans	1/2 tsp thyme
1 meaty ham bone	3/4 cup uncooked rice
large onion, finely chopped	8 oz smoked chorizo
4 sticks celery, thinly sliced	or similar sausage
1/2 red or green pepper, diced	2 tbsp corn oil
2 cloves garlic, crushed	1/2 cup water
bay leaf	Tabasco
1 tsp cumin	salt

Soak beans overnight and drain. Cover beans with cold water and cook on a high heat for 5 minutes. Drain and rinse. Cover with cold water and add ham bone and bring to a boil. Reduce heat and simmer 45 minutes. Beans will still be slightly underdone. Add onion, celery, pepper, garlic, bay leaf, cumin, thyme, and rice. Continue to cook for 30 minutes. Add more water if necessary.

Fry the sausage in corn oil on a medium heat. When cooked, remove with a slotted spoon and drain off most of the fat. Add water to pan and scrape up the bits left from cooking the sausage. Add to the soup. Remove meat from the ham bone, chopping it roughly; return the meat to the pot. Add Tabasco and salt to taste. The soup will be quite dry. Serve with Mexican Cornbread (see page 51).

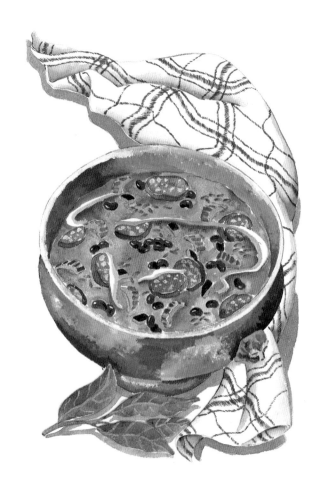

Barbecue Beans

Beans are said to have been the primary food eaten by the cowboy. This dish is especially good served in the shade of a tree with piles of beef cut from a side which has been roasting over charcoal all day.

---

1 1/2 cups navy beans	1/2 tsp black pepper
1 1/2 cups pinto beans	1 tbsp mustard powder
1 1/2 cups small butter beans	1 tbsp ground ginger
1 tsp salt	1/2 cup brown sugar
1/2 lb salt pork, in chunks	1/4 cup molasses
2 medium onions,	
coarsely chopped	

(serves 12)

Soak all beans overnight. Drain; bring to a boil in fresh water and cook for 5 minutes; drain, rinse, and return to boil and cook 30 minutes. Drain the partially cooked beans, reserving the liquid. Put 1/4 of the pork in the bottom of a very large casserole dish. Alternate layers of beans, onion and pork. Combine the remaining ingredients with 1/2 pint of the bean liquid and pour over the casserole. Top up with the remaining liquid. Cook at 250°F for 7–8 hours or until the beans are completely cooked. If the beans dry out, top up with the remaining bean liquid or hot water. The beans should not be too watery. Barbecue beans can be prepared ahead.

Fried Okra

The *Encyclopedia Larousse* suggests that okra should be soaked in water before use, but no Texas cook would dream of using anything but the fresh unsoaked pod. The vegetable appears in Southern, Cajun, and soul food recipes, but this is okra at its best, served on a hot summer's day accompanied by freshly baked bread, beans from the garden, and cold ham.

8 oz okra	1 tsp salt
1 oz plain flour	oil for cooking
1 oz cornmeal	

Wash the okra and cut off the top and tail if discolored. Cut into $1/2$" pieces. Mix the flour, cornmeal, and salt and coat the okra. Heat $1/2$" oil in skillet and cook okra until lightly browned.

Poppy Seed Dressing

Poppy seed dressing was first served over fruit salads in the Zodiac Room, the restaurant at the top of Dallas's Neiman Marcus. Though the original has never been revealed, this is a good rendering of it. Serve over a mixture of orange and grapefruit sections to make a Texas Cocktail.

1 tsp onion juice or	$1/2$ cup corn or groundnut oil
1 tbsp grated onion	(not olive oil)
3 tbsp superfine sugar	$1/4$ cup white wine vinegar
$1/2$ tsp dry mustard	$1/2$ tbsp poppy seed
$1/2$ tsp salt	

Mix together all the ingredients except the poppy seed. Add the poppy seed and check the seasoning. The dressing will keep for up to two weeks in the refrigerator.

Serve over a salad of red cabbage, avocado, and green seedless grapes or as a dressing for any mixed fruit salad.

Green Rice Casserole

Rice fields run along the Gulf coast from the Louisiana border to well southwest of Houston. The low swampy land is ideal for the crop and Texas is still a major rice producer. Green rice is especially good with Beef Brisket (see page 24).

$^3/_4$ *cup rice, cooked*	*I egg, beaten*
bunch fresh parsley, chopped	*6 oz can evaporated milk*
$^1/_2$ *cup cheddar cheese, grated*	$^1/_4$ *cup corn oil*
small onion, chopped	*I $^1/_2$ tsp salt*
$^1/_4$ *green pepper, chopped*	*juice and grated rind $^1/_2$ lemon*
clove garlic, minced	*I tsp paprika*

In a buttered I quart casserole dish, combine the rice, parsley, cheese, onion, pepper, and garlic. In a separate bowl, combine the remaining ingredients, except the paprika, and add to the rice mixture and blend well. Sprinkle with paprika. Bake at 350°F for I $^1/_2$ hours. Rice will be firm like a well-baked custard. The slightly burned bits around the edge are especially good. The rice warms up well the next day either in a microwave or a conventional oven.

Peach Pickles

Pickling and bottling were the lot of the Texas farm wife until the 1950s. Now the freezer has taken much of the work out of preserving the summer surplus. Peach pickles are well worth the extra effort; they make an unusual accompaniment to cold meats, especially ham.

---

12 ripe peaches
Syrup
1 1/4 cups cider vinegar
1 1/4 cups water
2 cups sugar
1 tsp ground cloves
12 whole cloves
2 cinnamon sticks, broken up
12 allspice berries

Dip peaches in boiling water for 30 seconds, then remove skins. Cool completely in cold water. Drain. Keep in a bath of cool water to which 1 tablespoon of salt has been added.

To make syrup, bring vinegar, water, sugar, and ground cloves to a boil, ensuring that the sugar dissolves. Add peaches and boil for about 5 minutes, or until peaches are tender when pierced with a fork. This timing will depend on ripeness of the peaches. Pack the peaches in hot, sterilized jars and keep

warm in a low-heated oven. Continue to cook the syrup and reduce it by one half. Pour over the peaches, dividing the whole cloves, cinnamon stick, and allspice berries among the jars; seal immediately. When the jars are cooled, test the seal. Store in a cool dark place.

San Jacinto Corn

This recipe commemorates the corn that General Sam Houston sent his army home with after the Battle of San Jacinto, which secured Texas independence. Each man was given the grain and told to go home, plant a crop, and build a nation.

4 ears corn	small onion, finely chopped
1/4 cup butter	1/2 tsp salt
1/4 red pepper, chopped	1/4 tsp white pepper
1/4 green pepper, chopped	

Husk corn and remove silk. Slice corn from cob with sharp knife. Use the back of a knife blade to scrape the milk from the cobs. Melt the butter in a small pan; add the corn and corn milk. Simmer for 3 minutes. Add the peppers, onion and seasonings and simmer for a further 3 minutes.

Spinach Salad

Popeye, that famous consumer of spinach, is commemorated in South Texas' Rio Grande Valley with a statue — there he stands with his tin of spinach squeezed open, looking over the spinach fields which surround him. This salad is good as a starter or as a main course at lunch.

---

1 lb young spinach leaves, washed and dried
3 eggs, boiled and chopped
4 oz button mushrooms, thinly sliced
6 rashers smoked streaky bacon, chopped and fried
bunch spring onions
vinaigrette or sweet/sour hot dressing
Vinaigrette
1/4 cup cider vinegar
4 tbsp oil
1 tsp dry mustard powder
1/2 tsp salt
Sweet/sour dressing
4 tbsp bacon fat
1 1/2 tbsp wine vinegar
1 tbsp brown sugar

Tear the spinach leaves into medium-size pieces into a salad bowl. Add the eggs, mushrooms, fried bacon and spring onions to the spinach. Dress with vinaigrette (mix together oil, vinegar, mustard and salt) or with a sweet/sour dressing made by heating 4 tbsp of the fat from the bacon and adding the wine

vinegar and brown sugar. Mix until sugar dissolves and pour over the salad. The spinach will wilt slightly. Serve immediately.

Squash Bake

Though called a bake, this dish is in truth a soufflé. Squash or gourds were a staple food of the Indians in pre-Columbian Texas. There is a huge variety of squash available in Texas, but try the yellow zucchini now available. It is much milder in taste than the green. Or try a small patty pan squash if it is available.

---

6 yellow zucchini, sliced
I tsp salt
$^5/_8$ cup sour cream
I egg, separated
I tbsp plain flour
$^3/_4$ cup grated cheddar cheese
3 rashers smoked streaky bacon, cooked crisp and then crumbled
$^1/_4$ cup dry white bread crumbs
I tbsp butter, melted

Oil a I quart casserole dish. Steam the zucchini for 4 minutes, until *al dente*. Mix salt, sour cream, egg yolk, and flour. Beat egg white stiffly and fold in the egg yolk mixture. Spread half of the squash in the bottom of the dish. Top with a layer of egg, then the cheese and bacon. Top second layer with bread crumbs and pour over the melted butter. Bake uncovered 20–25 minutes at 350°F; the top should be nicely browned.

Beef Brisket with Barbecue Sauce

Brisket is a tougher cut of beef than others and responds well to marinating. This quantity serves 12, but half the meat can be frozen in the cooking liquid and served later or used for sandwiches.

	6–7 lb brisket, rolled
Marinade	⁵/₈ cup beer or red wine
2 tsp onion salt	4 tbsp Worcestershire Sauce
1 tbsp celery salt	¹/₄ cup brown sugar
1 tsp garlic salt	1 – 1³/₄ lb can tomatoes,
3 tbsp Worcestershire Sauce	chopped
1¹/₄ cups lager or red wine	⁵/₈ cup lemon juice
Barbecue Sauce	Tabasco to taste
large onion, finely chopped	salt
¹/₂ cup butter	water

Prepare the marinade by mixing all the ingredients in a covered dish large enough to hold the brisket. Marinate overnight in a cool place. Turn the meat in the marinade at least once. To make the sauce, first brown the onions in the butter then add the remaining ingredients and simmer for 30 minutes. The sauce is best made ahead.

Cook the brisket, covered, in the marinade at 275°F for 45 minutes per pound. The brisket can be served hot at this point with the sauce, which can be either hot or cold. If the brisket is to be served cold, remove from the dish and set aside. The marinade and juices from the cooking can be reduced and used as an alternative to the barbecue sauce.

Buffalo Wings

The only buffalo this dish has been near is Buffalo, New York, where it originated. However, it features on many Texas restaurant menus as well as home party menus. The wings are good finger food and a relief from the ubiquitous party drumsticks.

---

1 1/2 lb chicken wings
1/4 cup butter, melted
2–3 tbsp West Indian Hot Pepper Sauce or Tabasco
Blue Cheese Dressing
1 1/4 cups mayonnaise
5/8 cup buttermilk
1/2 tbsp lemon juice
garlic clove, crushed
1/4 tsp lemon pepper or white pepper
3 oz blue cheese, crumbled

Split wings at joints. Spread wing pieces on a baking tray and bake at 325°F for 35 minutes. Remove chicken from tray to a bowl. Combine butter and hot sauce and coat the chicken with the mixture. Cool; then cover and refrigerate overnight. Before serving, spread on a tray and bake for 10 minutes at 425°F. Serve with blue cheese dressing for dipping.

To make the dressing, combine well all the ingredients except the cheese. Fold in the cheese and refrigerate. Any left over dressing can be used as a salad dressing or as a dip with crudités.

Chilli Con Carne

Chilli lovers pour into Terlingua, near Austin, on the first weekend in November for the Annual International Chilli Cookoff. A true Texas chilli has no beans and no tomatoes; the recipe below is an adaptation of a two-alarm chilli which once won in Terlingua.

medium onion, chopped	1–4 tsp chilli powder
clove garlic, crushed	(to taste)
1 tbsp corn oil	1 tbsp tomato purée
1 lb coarsely minced beef	14 oz can tomatoes
2–3 tsp ground cumin	salt to taste
2–3 tsp ground coriander	fresh coriander, chopped

Cook the onions and garlic until clear in the corn oil. Add beef and continue to cook, stirring to make sure meat is browned. Add cumin, coriander, chilli powder; cook for 2 minutes and add the tomato purée and tomatoes. Cover and cook over a low heat for 1 hour. If the chilli becomes too dry, add a little water. Check seasoning and add salt to taste.

Add 1/4 cup chopped fresh coriander. Serve with separate dishes of grated cheese, chopped onion and chopped fresh coriander. (This dish can be frozen when cool. Add coriander when defrosted and ready to serve.)

Fajitas

In the early nineteen eighties, no party in Texas was a party without a large dish of Fajitas. The best fajitas I've ever tasted were in El Paso. They were made with a combination of beef and chicken — a typically Mexican medley of meat and poultry.

---

1 1/2 lb skirt or flank steak
lemon pepper
1 1/4 cup lager or beer
1 cup vinaigrette (3/4 cup oil, 1/4 cup vinegar,
1/2 tsp salt, 1 tsp mustard)

Trim meat of all fat and membrane. Rub meat with lemon pepper. In a covered glass or ceramic bowl, combine the lager or beer and vinaigrette, add the meat, cover, and marinate overnight. To cook, either grill over very hot charcoal for 8 minutes per side or slice very thinly and cook quickly in a hot skillet that has been lightly oiled.

Serve with a combination of chunks of different colored peppers and onions which have been freshly cooked in a lightly oiled pan. White meat of chicken or turkey makes a tasty alternative to beef. Fajitas can be served with a spicy tomato sauce, flour tortillas, sour cream, and grated cheese.

King Ranch Chicken

The King Ranch is the biggest in Texas, equaling 1.23 Rhode Islands or 823,000 acres. Founded in 1853 by a former Rio Grande riverboat captain, it has no connection with this dish — except the name. Canned soup makes the dish quick but you can use instead 2 1/2 cups of white sauce using equal parts milk and chicken stock and adding 4 oz of cooked sliced mushrooms.

corn tortillas or tortilla chips	1 tsp ground cumin
1 lb cooked boned chicken	11 oz can cream of
5/8 cup chicken broth	mushroom soup
medium onion, finely chopped	11 oz can cream of
1/2 green pepper,	chicken soup
finely chopped	4 oz can tomatoes,
2 cups grated cheese,	drained and chopped
preferably Monterey Jack	4 tbsp canned chopped
2 tsp chilli powder	green chillies

(serves 8)

Cover the bottom of an 8" x 11" baking dish with tortillas or tortilla chips which have been dipped in chicken broth. Cut chicken into bite-size bits and spread over tortillas. Mix together the onion and pepper and distribute over chicken. Top with 1/2 of cheese. Sprinkle with chilli powder and ground cumin. Pour soups, then tomatoes and chillies on top. Cover with the remainder of the cheese. Bake uncovered at 350°F for 40 minutes. Cook half for eating immediately and freeze the other half.

Roast Quail with Rice

Farmed quail is now readily available; however, in the last century wild quail and most other game birds were plentiful all over the Texas plains. This dish will feed four very hungry people.

8 quail, cleaned	$^3/_4$ cup uncooked rice
$^3/_4$ cup butter	1$^1/_4$ cup chicken stock
medium onion, chopped	2 tbsp port
green pepper, chopped	salt, pepper
clove garlic, minced	

Sauté the quail in the butter and remove to a plate. Sauté the vegetables but do not allow to brown. Add the rice, chicken stock, and port and bring to a boil. Add salt and pepper to taste and pour into an oven-proof dish. Top with the quail, cover and cook at 350°F for 25 minutes. Raise the temperature to 400°F, uncover the dish and cook for a further 10 minutes or until the liquid is absorbed and the quail browned. You can use a combination of partially cooked wild rice and white rice.

Sausage Bake

Texas sausage is very spicy. Made with coarsely minced pork with herbs, spices and/or chillies added, the hotter it is the better it is.

1 lb coarsely minced pork	$^3/_4$ cup sugar

1 tsp crushed chillies	1 tbsp butter
2 cooking apples, thinly sliced	1 tbsp plain flour

Mix together pork and chillies. Spread this sausage mixture in an oven-proof dish. Top with sliced apples. Blend sugar, butter, and flour to make a crumb mixture and sprinkle over apples. Bake 1 hour at 375°F. Half way through the cooking time, drain any excess liquid from the dish.

Shrimp Gumbo

The word "Gumbo" is a corruption of gombo, meaning "okra", an essential ingredient in any gumbo. Cooked chicken or pork can be substituted for the shrimp. This dish has come across the state line from Louisiana which has Cajun and French cooking traditions.

2 tbsp corn oil	4 oz okra, cleaned, topped
3 rashers smoked streaky bacon	and sliced into 1/2" pieces
1 cup plain flour	1 large tomato, peeled
1 large onion, chopped	and chopped
1 clove garlic, chopped	bay leaf
2 1/2 qts cold water	2 tbsp red wine vinegar
2 sticks celery, sliced	Tabasco, to taste
1/2 green pepper, chopped	1 lb cooked shrimp

Chop the bacon and cook in oil for 3 minutes. Add onion and garlic and make a *roux* with the flour. Cook for at least 5 minutes. (The mixture will be dark brown.) After 5 minutes, slowly add the cold water, stirring to keep the flour mixture

from going lumpy. Then add t[...]
vinegar and simmer for 2 hours. [...]
burn. Just before serving, check th[...]
Tabasco. Add shrimp and just war[...]
be very thick and brown. Serve [...]

Berry Col[...]

The sides of the roads of Texas h[...]
berries and wild mustang grape vi[...]
two-crust pie is quick and a good [...]
of pastry.

---

6 oz shortcrust [...]
3 cups berries — blackberries, bluebe[...]
or a mixture of avail[...]
½ cup suga[...]
I tbsp plain fl[...]
I tsp ground cinn[...]
2 tbsp butte[...]
¼ tsp cinnamon and I tsp super[...]

Combine the fruit with the sugar, c[...]
into a I½ pint oven dish. Top the ber[...]
the pastry and cut into strips and m[...]
cobbler. Pour 2 oz water over the [...]
cinnamon/sugar mixture. Bake at [...]
until the pastry is cooked and the su[...]
crust on the top. Serve either with sw[...]
or ice cream.

A LITTLE **Texas** Cookbook

Carolyn Dehnel

ILLUSTRATED BY
SUE DRAY

Squashed Bake

Though called a bake, this dish is in truth a soufflé. Squash or
gourds were a staple food of the Indians in pre-Columbian
Texas. There is a huge variety of squash available in Texas,
but try the yellow zucchini now available. It is much milder
in taste than the green. Or try a small patty pan squash if it
is available.

6 yellow zucchini, sliced
I tsp salt
½ cup sour cream
I egg, separated
I tbsp plain flour
¾ cup grated cheddar cheese
3 rashers smoked streaky bacon, cooked crisp and then crumbled
¼ cup dry white bread crumbs
I tbsp butter, melted

Oil a I quart casserole dish. Steam the zucchini for 4 minutes,
until *al dente*. Mix salt, sour cream, egg yolk, and flour. Beat
egg white stiffly and fold in the egg yolk mixture. Spread half
of the squash in the bottom of the dish. Top with a layer of
egg, then the cheese and bacon. Top second layer with bread
crumbs and pour over the melted butter. Bake uncovered 20–
25 minutes at 350°F; the top should be nicely browned.

Chronicle Books

Buttermilk Pie

Buttermilk nowadays isn't the same as when it was the remains of the buttermaking by the farmer's wife. But the pie is still delicious. For a real country lunch, serve with mashed potatoes, fresh vegetables from the garden and finish off with buttermilk pie à la mode.

2 cups sugar	3 tbsp lemon juice
2 tbsp plain flour	1 tsp vanilla essence
1/4 tsp nutmeg	1 tsp grated lemon rind
1/2 cup butter, melted	9" pie shell, baked
3 eggs, lightly beaten	blind for 12 minutes
1 cup buttermilk	

Mix sugar, flour, and nutmeg. Add the melted butter and mix. Stir in the remaining ingredients and mix well. Pour into the pie shell and bake for 1 hour at 350°F. Test for doneness after 45 minutes. If done, a knife inserted into the center will come out clean.

Cheat's Banana Pecan Ice Cream

Pecans grow all over Texas, but especially along the Brazos River Valley. They have a more delicate flavor than walnuts but can be used any time that walnuts are called for.

1 1/2 pts good quality commercial vanilla ice cream
3 ripe bananas

½ cup chopped pecans
extra roasted pecans for garnish

Soften the ice cream in a large bowl. Thoroughly mash the bananas and add with the pecans to the softened ice cream. Mix thoroughly and return to the freezer. Serve garnished with chopped roasted pecans.

Chocolate Pecan Pie

Pecan pie is a traditional southern dish. All chocolate lovers will welcome the addition of their favorite ingredient. Use either light or dark corn syrup — whichever you can find.

³/₄ cup sugar
1 cup corn syrup
½ tsp salt
2 tbsp plain flour
3 eggs, beaten
2 tbsp butter, melted
3 oz unsweetened chocolate, melted
1½ tsp vanilla essence
2 cups pecans
9" pie shell, baked blind for 10 minutes

Combine the sugar, corn syrup, salt, flour, and eggs in a bowl and mix well. Fold in the remaining ingredients. Pour into the pie shell and bake for 25–40 minutes at 350°F until a knife inserted in the center comes out clean. Begin to test after 25 minutes. The top can overbake and dry out, so the last 15 minutes are critical. Use walnuts if pecans are not available.

Hummingbird Cake

This moist, rich cake is popular throughout the South. It makes a good party dessert baked in a 13" x 9" pan and frosted.

3 cups plain flour
2 cups sugar
1 tsp baking powder
1 tsp salt
1 tsp ground cinnamon
3 eggs, beaten
1 cup corn oil
1½ tsp vanilla essence
8 oz can crushed pineapple, undrained

1 cup chopped pecans or walnuts
3–4 bananas, mashed to make up 2 cups

Frosting
8 oz cream cheese, softened
½ cup butter
1 lb confectioner's sugar
1 tsp vanilla essence
½ cup finely chopped pecans or walnuts

(serves 10–12)

Combine the first five ingredients in a large bowl. Add eggs and oil; mix until dry ingredients are moistened. Stir in vanilla, pineapple, nuts, and bananas. Spoon batter into three 9 inch cake pans which have been oiled and floured. Bake at 350°F for 25–30 minutes or until a toothpick inserted in center comes out clean. Cool in pans for 15 minutes. Turn onto cooling racks and allow to cool completely.

To make frosting, combine cream cheese and butter and beat until smooth. Add confectioner's sugar and vanilla; beat until light and fluffy. Spread frosting between layers and on top and sides of cake. Sprinkle top with chopped nuts.

Jeff Davis' Favorite Chess Pie

Jefferson Davis was President of the Confederacy, but he is best remembered in Texas as the man who, before the Civil War, as U.S. Secretary of War, introduced camels to West Texas as beasts of burden for the Army. The idea never caught on.

---

1 1/2 cups sugar
2 eggs, beaten
1/2 cup creamy milk
1 tbsp flour
1/2 tsp vanilla essence
1/4 cup butter, melted
1/2 cup sweet coconut
1/2 cup pecan or walnut halves
10" pie plate lined with short pastry

Beat sugar, eggs, milk, flour, vanilla, and butter until well mixed. Stir in coconut and nuts and pour into pie shell. Bake for 45 minutes to 1 hour at 350°F. Check pie after 3/4 hour; the pie is done when a knife inserted into the center comes out clean. Serve with vanilla ice cream or sweetened whipped cream.

Peanut Cookies

Peanuts, also known as goobers, are a miracle of nature, a legume which has more than a thousand uses. Hundreds of thousands of acres are planted in Texas for human and cattle consumption. This is an old recipe from a very old newspaper — probably the *Texas Farmer's Weekly*.

---

1 cup butter
1 1/2 cups brown sugar
2 eggs, lightly beaten
2 tsp vanilla essence
3 cups plain flour
1/2 tsp bicarbonate soda
1 tsp salt
2 cups salted peanuts
(makes 60)

Cream butter, sugar, eggs, and vanilla thoroughly. Sieve together the flour, soda, and salt and add the creamed mixture. Mix in the peanuts. Drop by teaspoons onto lightly oiled baking sheets. Press the dough down with the tines of a fork which have been dipped in flour. Cook 8–10 minutes at 375°F until golden. Cookies will be crisp.

Mexican Corn Bread

The corndodger, or corncake, helped win the West. It went in a cowboy's saddlebag and kept for weeks; it was carried by the Confederate soldier into battle. Made of cornmeal and water, with a little salt for the lucky, it was then fried on a griddle. How envious the cowboy and the soldier would be of Mexican corn bread!

---

4 oz can green chillies
1 cup cornmeal
$^1/_2$ tsp salt
10 $^1/_2$ oz can cream-style corn
2 eggs
$^5/_8$ cup buttermilk
$^1/_2$ tsp bicarbonate soda
$^1/_3$ cup shortening
1 cup grated cheddar cheese

Drain and chop the chillies. Reserve. Mix remaining ingredients, except the cheese, until just moistened. Pour $^1/_2$ the mixture into an oiled 9" pie pan or plate. Cover with chopped chillies and cheese then cover with remaining mixture. Bake at 375°F for 35–40 minutes, until cooked and well browned.

Variation: In addition to cheese and chillies in the center, add 12oz beef mince which has been cooked with a small chopped onion and seasoned with ground cumin. Serve as main course with a green salad.

Peach Muffins

Although peaches may be more associated with Georgia than Texas, there are still thousands of acres of peach orchards across the state. Farmers' markets in towns are filled with the aroma of bushel baskets for sale. These muffins are good for breakfast, for mid-morning break, or with tea.

---

1 egg
1 cup whole milk
3 tbsp butter, melted
$^2/_3$ cup sugar
$^1/_2$ tsp salt
1 tsp lemon juice
$^1/_4$ tsp vanilla essence
2 cups plain flour
3 tsp baking powder
$^1/_4$ tsp cinnamon
2 medium peaches, washed and chopped (unskinned)
(makes 24)

Beat egg. Stir in the milk, butter, sugar, salt, lemon juice, vanilla. Sift together flour, baking powder, cinnamon. Stir into milk mixture until just moistened. Do not overmix. Fold in peaches. Fill oiled muffin pans until $^2/_3$ full. Bake at 450°F for 20 minutes, or until lightly browned. They are best eaten on the day they are baked. They can be frozen and kept for 1 month. Warm gently after defrosting.

Bourbon Drinks

Although Bourbon comes from Bourbon County, Kentucky, it is still very much associated with the Texas cowboy and the saloon — the drink one hears ordered in those innumerable cowboy moves seen every Saturday at the Kid Show at the local cinema.

Cowboys

2 parts bourbon
I part double cream
freshly ground nutmeg

Combine bourbon with cream in a cocktail shaker filled with ice. Shake and strain into glasses that have been kept in the freezer for at least an hour. Grate nutmeg over top.

Indians

2 parts bourbon
I part dry vermouth
dash bitters

Combine bourbon, vermouth and bitters in a cocktail shaker filled with ice. Shake to mix and strain into icy cocktail glasses.

Texas Lemonade

Texas lemonade has a kick like a bronco. Serve it the frontier way — from a Mason jar over ice. Bourbon or white rum can be substituted.

12 lemons	carbonated water
1/2 cup superfine sugar	vodka

Squeeze the lemons into a measuring jug. Add the sugar to the juice and stir until it is dissolved. Add water to make half as much again. Pour into ice-filled glasses. Top with one measure of vodka. Garnish with lemon slices.

Texas Wine Cooler

Wine was produced in Texas from the time of the Spanish until Prohibition. In the last 25 years production has begun again. One of the major producing areas is in the Big Bend Country around Fort Stockton. This cooler is lighter and more interesting than a straightforward spritzer. To make it a true Texas Cooler, use Texas wine and oranges.

bottle Texas white wine, well chilled
freshly squeezed orange juice
slices of orange

Fill each glass one third full of wine; top up with orange juice. Garnish with orange slices.

Sun Tea

Gallons of iced tea are drunk on hot summer days in Texas. This version is very easy to make and doesn't have the "brewed" taste which comes from using boiling water and tea. Serve Sun Tea in tall glasses and enjoy it — even if the summer isn't all that hot.

---

6 tea bags
3 lt/3 ¹/₂ qts cold water
sugar to taste
mint leaves
lemon slices

Place the tea bags in a one-gallon jar and add the cold water. Cap the jar loosely and place it in a sunny spot for 3 hours. Remove the tea bags and sweeten to taste with sugar. Garnish with mint and/or lemon slice.

Index